Trust Based ENTREPRENEUR

Proven Ways to Pursue Opportunity and Reduce YOUR Risk.

For publishing consideration:
markgivenseminars@gmail.com

ISBN:
Paperback — 978-1-7370755-0-9

TESTIMONIALS AND ENDORSEMENTS

"This powerful, practical book is loaded with proven ideas and strategies you can use to get better results immediately."

—**Brian Tracy,** Brian Tracy International

"Mark's Strategies can change your life."

—**Kevin Harrington,** Original Shark on the hit TV Show "Shark Tank" and Inventor of the Infomercial ($5 Billion in Sales on TV)

"A business philosophy based on Trust — what an excellent idea! Mark is ahead of his time, or more accurately, he is right on time. This is what the world is clamoring for. Nicely done, sir!"

—**John David Mann,** coauthor of the classic bestseller ***The Go-Giver and The Go-Giver Series of books***

"I love and trust Mark and I know he can deliver on teaching your organization how to achieve more success by following his Trust Based Philosophy."

—**Jack Canfield,** Co-Creator, #1 NY Times Best-Selling Book Series Chicken Soup for the Soul®

"Leadership in today's world requires many things; most important amongst them is ***Trust***. Mark will give you a simplified look at how ***trust*** works while at the same time stimulating your thinking such that you will be able to implement the ideas that fit into your philosophy."

—**Kevin Eastman,** LA Clippers VP of Basketball Operations and Nike Consultant

"Mark Givens' book on ***Trust*** will motivate you to reach the next level in your personal development."

—**Rudy Ruettiger,** the MAN who inspired the hit movie "Rudy"

"Having known Mark Given for 20 years, I know he lives his philosophy of ***TRUST*** Based Leadership, Sales and Success every day. He has shared that knowledge with you in this book."

—**Zan Monroe,** CEO, Author, Speaker and Coach

"There are writers and speakers and then there are teachers. My good friend Mark is a teacher. He has captured the essence of the most critical aspect of relationships in a way that made me reflect on my own life and leadership. This short read has long-term impact. Thank you Mark for compiling such profound information on a ***Trust Based Philosophy***."

—**Jackie Leavenworth,** Author, International speaker, Trainer and Business Coach

"My friend, Mark Given has created his life and business based on building ***Trust***. Now you have an amazing opportunity to learn his Trust Based Philosophy. Read his book.....it can change your life!"

—**Jo Mangum,** Coach, Trainer, Author of The Strategic Agent®

"Mark lives his life by the values he shares about ***Trust***. This book will not only show you how to build ***Trust***, but how to use it and apply the principles in your everyday life. This book is a must read!"

—**Lee Barrett,** Author, Tutor, National Real Estate Instructor, Broker

"I've not only had the privilege of seeing Mark teach but also taught alongside him so I know firsthand that as a teacher and author his message is engaging ... genuine ... and, impactful! If you have not yet had the "Mark experience" this is a must read."

—**Ed Hatch,** International NLP Speaker,
Author, Coach - Negotiation Expert

"Having worked with Mark in business and volunteer situations, he has my complete ***Trust***. His books share discoveries and techniques that are easy to understand and implement immediately."

—**Pat Zaby,** REALTOR® and Highly Respected
National Speaker and Teacher

"***Trust*** Mark to create strategies that can be immediately implemented by everyone!"

—**Frank Serio,** Past National President–
Council of Residential Specialists

"Mark has provided for us an excellent resource to apply what we know is needful for ***Trust***. I love his list of concepts to make ourselves more trustworthy. The beauty in this book is in asking yourself the questions he provides and adding thoughtful answers to lock the concept into your regular practice of leading."

—**Monica Neubauer,** Speaker, Podcaster

"Mark is a Master Teacher and his Trust Based Philosophy has the power to improve lives and businesses."

—**Larry Kendall,** Author of Ninja Selling

Mark Blaine Given, Jr.
Testimonials and Recommendations

"From the first time you meet Blaine, you know he is a man of his word. He was born into a family of entrepreneurs and helping others with innovative products and services is part of his DNA. You can believe what Blaine has written in this book because he has experienced it all. I have seen first-hand how Blaine set's big goals and works tirelessly to achieve them both as a business owner and professional certified coach."

—**Matt Kersey,** Ph.D., PCC - President,
Transition States Coaching and Training

"It's long been communicated that people like to do business with those whom they know, like, and trust. Getting known and being liked come easy for most. But to be trusted is a weightier proposition. Trust requires a deep connection, not just to our clients, but also to ourselves. As a coach, Blaine knows that building trust requires attention and, intention. Trust-based entrepreneurship carries the weight off genuineness, authenticity, and accountability. Mark Blaine Given Jr opens our eyes, to the practical ways of becoming a trust-based entrepreneur."

—**Sackeena Gordon-Jones,** Ph.D., Master Certified Coach, and author of 'The Art and Practice of Transformational Leadership'

"Blaine has been a friend among friends to me personally. I grew up next door to Mark and Blaine, and I was able to witness firsthand how they lived and breathed these exact 'Trust Based Leadership' ideas that are the basis for this book. Blaine and Mark partnering on this book only confirms my belief and trust in them to provide outstanding, executable ideas. Trust what you read in this book and it can change your life!"

—**Preston McElheney,** President & CEO of Halifax Linen Inc

"Blaine is dedicated and responsive to my leadership needs and goals. Working with him is a pleasure, and it's productive!"

—**Martha Larson,** Director at Davidson Davie Community College Small Business Center

"Blaine has a talent for helping others see potential in themselves that they can't always see in themselves. He lives what he teaches and sincerely wants to help people reach whatever goals they set for themselves."

—**Lars Latimer,** Director of Business Development Logan River Academy

"I highly recommend Blaine. He has a knack for listening to my present problem but then working the true problem out of me as we talk. He knew how to pull those solutions right out of me."

—**Joel Harper,** General Business Counselor Small Business Technology University of North Carolina at Chapel Hill Keynote, Speaking, Teaching, and Coaching Testimonials and Endorsements

"If you are looking for a speaker, trainer and coach that can empower, inspire, and motivate your group then you must book my friend Mark Given!"

—**James Malinchak,** Featured on ABC's "Secret Millionaire", Best Selling Author of 20 Books

"We hire Mark to share his Trust Based Philosophy in leadership, sales and success with our 1500 members every year!"

—**Zan Monroe,** CEO Long Leaf Pine Association, Author, Speaker and Coach

"You are simply an event planners dream! I have been involved with contracting hundreds of speakers for various programs over the last 24+ years and I consider Mark as an exemplary example of an ideal speaker."

—**Rebecca Fletcher,** Director, GIRE – VP of Education

"My reason for inviting you back time and time again is purely selfish...it makes me look good. I thank you for the time you invest in crafting your message to meet our specific needs. I thank you for the energy you pump into our company. And, I thank you for your friendship. You are a class act that is very good at what you do. I look forward to our continued relationship and am anxious to have you back soon!"

—**Kit Hale,** Principal Broker/
Managing Partner MKB, REALTORS

A MESSAGE TO YOU FROM MARK AND MARK BLAINE, JR!

Every day, ***just like you***, each of us strive to be our best and focus on making a positive difference in this wonderful world.

You want to SUCCEED, help your family, be a good friend, make a secure living and be remembered as someone that can be ***trusted***. We want that too!

You already know that building or rebuilding **Trust** is a top priority for individuals and companies looking to sell more products, serve more people and capture their markets.

Trust is a critical link to all good relationships whether personal or professional.

Trust is a primary factor in how people work together effectively, build powerful relationships and listen to one another.

Lack of **Trust** creates poor productivity, low energy and reduced success.

So, in this important book, you'll learn how to build **Trust** in many ways and do it more often as you build your entrepreneurial opportunities.

You'll learn how to lead by example, communicate more openly, take responsible action and create more personal success by improving your **ENTREPRENUERIAL** skills.

Read this book. Then…share it with a friend. They **Trust** your opinion.

And, thank-you for taking the time to INVEST IN YOURSELF AND IN YOUR FUTURE! You never lose when you are striving to learn.

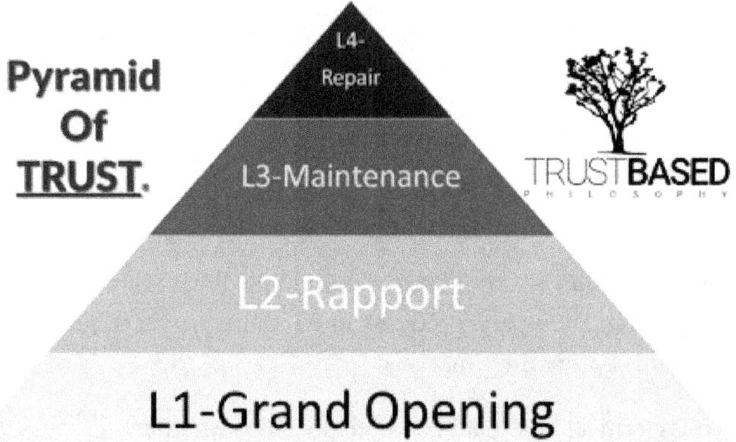
Pyramid
Of
TRUST.
L4-
Repair
L3-Maintenance
L2-Rapport
L1-Grand Opening
TRUSTBASED
PHILOSOPHY

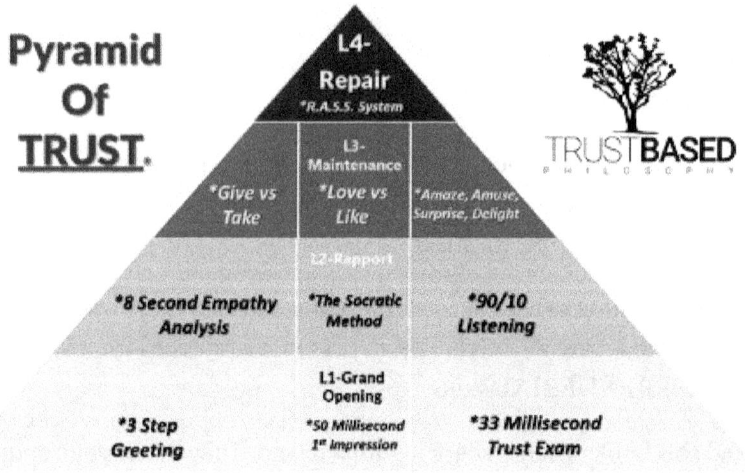
Pyramid
Of
TRUST.
L4-
Repair
*R.A.S.S. System
L3-
Maintenance
*Give vs
Take
*Love vs
Like
*Amaze, Amuse,
Surprise, Delight
L2-Rapport
*8 Second Empathy
Analysis
*The Socratic
Method
*90/10
Listening
L1-Grand
Opening
*3 Step
Greeting
*50 Millisecond
1st Impression
*33 Millisecond
Trust Exam
TRUSTBASED
PHILOSOPHY

DEDICATION

Mark B. Given Jr.

It has been said that behind every great man is a better woman! That statement is the epitome of my life and my "Mary Poppins" wife, Janelle. Everything good in my life is because of her! She makes me want to be better every day so that we can achieve and succeed in life, together! Our children Lee, Jacklyn, Bella, and Bolton cause me to pause and wonder how I can be so blessed! I am so grateful for their unique personalities and their love that makes me look forward to the future and the eternities. I was blessed with the most amazing parents any southern boy could ever want. Dad and mom sacrificed immensely for me and my siblings. They set an amazing example of what love is to a simple-minded child and how to succeed in the most important things in life. Dad and mom have experienced great success and it is because they live with the mantra that "no success can compensate for failure in the home!" Man, I am a lucky man! How many sons get to write a book with their dad? It has been my goal to be the kind of man both my Heavenly Father and earthly Father would be proud of. My Father in Heaven and His perfect Son, Jesus Christ, have given me more than any imperfect man should ever have. I strive daily to be deserving of the blessings that constantly poor into my life. I am so grateful for all the amazing mentors, confidants, and friends that have crossed my path and have made it better. "Because I knew you, I have been changed for good!" *"For Good" Wicked* I look forward to the many pathways and influences that are yet ahead. To all this and these I dedicate this book!

Mark Given

It is with profound admiration, respect and love that I dedicate this book and all that I do personally and professionally to my wonderful wife Janice, our sons Blaine, Chase, Kyle, and Taylor, our daughter Kerri, our daughters-in-law Janelle, Bonnie, Lauren, and Gabbie and our son-in law Dylan, as well as our growing crop of beautiful and gifted grandchildren (now at 9). Without them, my life and work would be incomplete, and I would not know the joy I have experienced nearly every day of my life. Through the years, I have learned and grown because of many master teachers and speakers that have inspired me. Some know who they are, and some don't, but nonetheless, I thank each of you. Most of all today, I'd also like to thank my son Blaine. He has always been a gem and I'm so grateful to have had the opportunity to write this book with him.

And…without reservation, I thank my Heavenly Father and His Son, Jesus Christ, of which I know, none of the positive events or decisions I have experienced in my life would have been possible. THEY have proven over and over to me that nearly everything good is possible with <u>Focus</u> and <u>Determination</u> followed by <u>ACTION</u>!

CONTENTS

PROVEN WAY #1

ENTREPRENEUR – NOUN OR VERB?

entrepreneur

/ɒntrəprəˈnəː/

noun

1. a person who sets up a business or businesses, taking on financial risks in the hope of profit.

That is the definition you'll find online or in a dictionary, but is that what an Entrepreneur really is…a noun…someone who is only seeking profit?

I don't think so and that's clearly not what I believe (and I think I have the right, the knowledge and the experience to refute that definition because I've lived my entire adult life as an Entrepreneur, beginning way back in my mid 20's).

Let me take you back quickly with the cliff notes version.

Sometime during the year 1980 (the same year our oldest son Blaine was born…yep…that is the same Blaine that is co-writing this book), my visionary father-in-law, F. Lee Jones asked me to join with him and open a video and electronic store.

Video cassette recorders were new to market and electronic companies like JVC and Sony were positioning themselves with their version of what they believed was the new home entertainment sensation (of course you likely will remember that VHS won over BetaMax).

Lee had a unique ability to see potential and opportunity and wanted to invest heavily in VHS. He had the financial stability to invest, but what he lacked was the desire to sell, and he knew that no matter what the item or product, someone must sell it!

So…Lee made me an offer I could not resist, and we began, long before Wayne Hyzenga created the dynasty that we knew as Blockbuster Video.

We got in before Wayne and we got out before Wayne (that was actually pretty brilliant).

Lee put up the money and I delivered on the sales and relationship skills. He was already an Entrepreneur and the day we opened that first store…I became one.

That single event changed my entire life and it led to nearly 50 retail locations and 20 years of sweat and equity…I have never regretted it!

But…how does any of that apply to YOU?

Well…it proves that if I can do it, you can too.

I am not that smart, but I have a desire to work hard, watch trends, learn from others, and reposition. Over and over again.

And if that is YOU…please join in!

Being an Entrepreneur is not just a noun…it is quite definitely a verb.

Entrepreneurship takes action…everyday action!

And if you do it the way most successful Entrepreneurs do it, you will be consumed with it…but in a good way.

It is something you'll focus on constantly…it will burn within your soul.

Even as I write these words (I'm on a cruise ship in South America), the work continues along...and with a burning desire to make big things happen.

Every day, every week, every month and every year.

It's fun...it's exciting...it's scary...and most of all, it's rewarding!

And the best part is that you can still have harmony and balance in your family life, your religious life and your social life.

Isn't that why you would choose to do it in the first place?

FREEDOM baby...FREEDOM!

Entrepreneurship gives me everything I could have ever wanted my life to be.

Only God, Me and Gigi determine MY destiny...now how cool is that!

"You are the Michelangelo of your own life. The David that you are sculpting is YOU. And you do it with your thoughts."

—Joe Vitale, American Entrepreneur and Self-Help Author

If YOU chose to be an Entrepreneur today, what would you want to sell (you will be selling something – an idea, a product, a service, a system)?

TRUST BASED
PHILOSOPHY

We're so excited about opening our new business...
It's more thrilling than we could have ever imagined!

PROVEN WAY #2

WHY BE AN ENTREPRENEUR

You might have the same question many others have?

Why choose to be an Entrepreneur?

Isn't it easier to know that you'll be paid by someone else that's willing to take the risk…I'm just too afraid to do that?

To me though, there is only one amazingly simple answer to that "why" question…so…I will repeat it again!

Freedom Baby…FREE-DOM*!*

Freedom to choose your own career path. Freedom to control your calendar and your schedule. Freedom to make whatever amount of money you believe is enough. Freedom to go where you want to go and be there when you want to be there. Freedom to create YOUR destiny and YOUR legacy.

So…in reverse, my question to you has to be…

"What's holding you back?"

If you're working for somebody else (a company, an association or an individual) and you're dreaming about having more freedom to choose when and where you work, then "*what's holding you back*?"

If you are working for somebody else and you're not making the kind of money you think you're worth and you know you never will see that opportunity, then "*what's holding you back*?"

If you are working for someone else and you're missing out on those important family events like your kid's ballgames or school plays or dance recitals, or go to church with them, then "*what's holding you back*?"

If you are working for somebody else and you do not feel like you're making a difference, then "*what's holding you back*?"

If you are working for somebody else and you don't have the opportunity to do your best work and have the opportunity to immerse yourself in a favorite hobby, then "*what's holding you back*?"

If you're working for somebody else and you know there is something better out there for you…then…

"*What's holding you back*?"

Now's the perfect time!

There has never been a better time!

Money is available to get you started.

The world clamors for new products, ideas and better, simpler ways to do everything.

If you've ever thought about becoming an Entrepreneur, RIGHT NOW may just be the best time you'll ever see to make that choice…so get to it*!*

"Don't let the fear of the time it will take to accomplish something stand in the way of your doing it. The time will pass anyway; we might just as well put that passing time to the best possible use."

—Earl Nightingale

What's holding you back (go ahead...be bold enough to make that list right now)?

TRUST BASED
COACHING

PROVEN WAY #3

7 CHARACTERISTICS OF SUCCESSFUL ENTREPRENEURS

1. A Passion and a Desire to Win–You cannot guess here. You must have something so important to you that when things get tough (and things will get tough), you won't let anyone, or anything talk you into giving up.
2. Self-Motivation – You have got to have the strength, habits, and willpower to get up every day and do something that will help you achieve the success you are seeking. If you are the kind of person that requires an alarm clock every morning to get you where you need to be on schedule, or a boss that has to tell you exactly what to do in order for you to get things done, Entrepreneurship is likely not your calling!
3. A Product or Service that Someone Will Want to Buy – you cannot create it until you know what it is and if you create it, someone out there in the world must have a need for what you created. Do not guess here! Be really really clear on how your product or service is going to fit in the marketplace and how your product or service is better than the competition.
4. You Either Need to Have Great Networking and Selling Skills or You Have to Have Someone on Your Team that Does – read my book ***Trust Based Networking-Proven Ways to Stop Meeting and Start Connecting*** and my book ***Trust Based Selling-Proven Ways to Stop Selling and Start Attracting*** and you will understand what I am talking about here. Somebody (either you or someone on your team) must sell your product or system or idea or service, and if you are lousy at selling and communicating, you better get someone who isn't!

5. You Have to Be Willing to Take Some Risks – entrepreneurship is all about taking risks. And, in my mind it rates right up there with cliff diving, wire walking and skyscraper building (and I'm pretty afraid of heights!). If you are adverse to taking daily risks, you'll be much better off working for someone that will.
6. Time and Money Management Skills – let me just take you down a path of being honest with yourself about your habits. If money burns a hole in your pocket and you cannot easily see a bigger picture when it comes to making and spending money, successful entrepreneurship may be out of your reach. If you struggle maintaining your daily and weekly calendar and you never can seem to get to places or appointments on time, entrepreneurship may not work for you.
7. Flexibility – I am pretty rigid at times, but in a good way (although Gigi might argue that at times). Entrepreneurs recognize that things can change fast. Sometimes priorities that you believed were unmovable have changed. Often times, people don't perform on their promises…and it sometimes feels like there are a thousand other things that will be out of your control. But…when you're flexible, miracles will happen!

"You already have every characteristic necessary for success if you recognize, claim, develop and use them."

Zig Ziglar

Of the Seven Characteristics of an **Entrepreneur**, which one is your greatest strength? On which one do you need the most improvement?

TRUST BASED
ACADEMY

PROVEN WAY #4

ENTREPRENEURS ARE FOCUSED

I've spent my life watching and learning from successful Entrepreneurs and cataloged steps to their success.

Entrepreneurs come in all shapes and sizes.

Entrepreneurs come from many diverse backgrounds and cultures.

What's most interesting is that Entrepreneurial people, regardless of their history have a couple of important and copy-able traits.

You might even like to know what they are?

#1–A vision of what they want.

#2–A focus that deters them from distractions.

#3–A clear reality of "WHY" they are driven to make it happen.

#4–An understanding that there is a difference between a goal and a priority...

1. Goals are the foundation for actionable steps.
2. Priorities keep you glued to those steps and help you get to the finish line.

5–A willingness to make mistakes and still press on.

6–The wisdom to ask for help.

You may or may not be a Dr. Phil fan, but he made a statement that is particularly valid here.

Dr. Phil said: ***"The only difference between you and someone you envy is that you settled for less."***

To me…it is all about focus…so go get to work and stay focused!

"Spend eighty percent of your time focusing on the opportunities of tomorrow rather than the problems of yesterday."

Brian Tracy

What are three steps you could take today to help you focus on your Entrepreneurial goal?

TRUST BASED
PHILOSOPHY

PROVEN WAY #5

ENTREPRENEURS ARE COMPETITIVE

We are already competing at something every day.

We cannot avoid it.

The only way not to be caught up in some sort of competition is to not participate in life and that does not usually work out very well.

The difference between Entrepreneurs and non-entrepreneurs is in their willingness to compete on a different playing field.

So…if you seek to go down the Entrepreneurial path, hone in on these nine priorities to help you improve your competitive advantage and win more often:

1. Think…What do I do ***better*** than anyone else?
2. What ***qualities*** do I offer that make me ***irresistible***?
3. How can I save people ***time***?
4. How can I save people ***money***?
5. How can I make people feel ***better*** about themselves or their circumstances?
6. What ***valuable*** services do I offer that my competitor doesn't or won't?
7. Can I statistically ***prove*** it?

8. What ***statements*** do/will my clients use to persuade others of my competitive advantage?
9. What ***strategic plan*** do I have to continually seek improvement?

To be totally realistic, you might as well embrace the reality of competition anyway because the moment you begin to succeed, copycats will appear (the highest form of compliment).

Get ready for competition…it's an every-day occurrence*!*

"The competition is often just as good (or better) than you, so the only real competitive instrument available to you is to learn to be better, not just merely louder."

Mark Given

What product, idea or service am I prepared to offer that will get me in the game, and allow me to compete?

Bring it on Nabisco!

PROVEN WAY #6

ENTREPRENEURS ARE DETERMINED

We have all seen it (just watch the news for 5 minutes).

Things do not always work out the way we want, and bad things sometimes happen to really good people.

But…when they are Determined, good people overcome bad things.

How do they do it?

I always carry a little pad in my pocket wherever I go, and recently during some trials and a tough day, I wrote a new thought in my little book which goes like this…

"Through dedicated focus and forgiveness, weak things become strong."

I really believe that is true and I have witnessed it over and over in my lifetime.

It is only through conscious effort that we overcome our significant challenges…it takes Determination.

In a 2012 Huffington blog post, Linda Durnell wrote…

"I believe each of us has an innate capacity for strength and throughout our lives, we develop — through conditions we find ourselves in — the skills to be secure, passionate, formidable and Determined."

It's through those difficult challenges that we grow…so when bad things happen to you…refocus and get more Determined.

Now you may have had enough bad things happen in your life (or in your business) that you're starting to feel like you should be a giant, so if that's you…look down on us little people and give us your hand… teach us what you've learned.

The world will benefit from your knowledge and wisdom, but only if you reach down and pull us up!

"Nothing in the world can take the place of Persistence and Determination. Talent will not; nothing is more common than unsuccessful men with talent. Genius will not; unrewarded genius is almost a proverb. Education will not; the world is full of educated derelicts. Persistence and Determination alone is omnipotent. The slogan "Press On" has solved and always will solve the problems of the human race."

Calvin Coolidge

Beginning today, what steps could you take to increase your levels of Determination?

TRUST BASED
ACADEMY

PROVEN WAY #7

ENTREPRENEURS ARE CREATIVE

Several years back, I came across a Harvard University blog post written by Warren Berger.

I am sure glad I saved it.

Warren's thought fits perfectly with what has been on my mind as I contribute to this Trust Based Philosophy book.

I have paraphrased Warren Berger's thoughts today but have copied the original link at the bottom so you can read his words in more depth if you would like.

Here is what I found in his post…

Say this with me: How might we?

This is a phrase that many organizations and companies should use immediately to tackle challenges creatively.

How "might" we improve X ... or completely re-imagine Y... or find a new way to accomplish Z?

This approach to innovation ensures that you're asking the right questions and steering clear of more limiting inquiries like "How can we?" or "How should we?" which imply judgment.

Instead, "How might we" helps people think of options more freely and opens up possibilities.

The "How" assumes there are solutions out there…it provides creative confidence.

"Might" implies that it's OK to put any idea on the table…it might work and/or it might not.

And the "We" signals that we are all going to work together and build on one another's strengths and ideas.

I'm not sure about you, but I think it's brilliant and amazing that just a few simple words might, can or will open up so many new possibilities.

Just the clarity of changing those words caused me to put up a new dry erase board on my office door that has helped me begin the creative exchange of new ideas and actions.

I Love It*!*

Begin and continue the process of creativity by considering "How Might We".

It "Might" just make an amazing

"Our thinking creates a pathway to success or failure"

Mark Given

What am I working on right now that by changing the words *"how should we"* to *"how might we"* will create new possibilities and entirely different results?

TRUST BASED
COACHING

PROVEN WAY #8

ENTREPRENEURS ARE CONFIDENT

You may have only a bit of competence...but add Confidence and you will win.

You may lack knowledge...but add Confidence and you'll look like you know.

You may not yet have the skills...but add Confidence and you will look like a pro.

You may be in a heavy fog and feel lost or disoriented...but adding Confidence will give you the clarity to see.

YOU can take my word on it...go get more Confidence and watch your competence grow!

"We hold ourselves back in ways both big and small, by lacking self-confidence, by not raising our hands, and pulling back when we should be leaning in."

Sheryl Sandberg

TRUST BASED
PHILOSOPHY

Now that you've made the decision to either become an Entrepreneur or improve your Entrepreneurial endeavor, list the things that are holding you back because you lack the confidence to move forward?

I'm thrilled to now introduce my oldest son Blaine.

He has always been a willing creative thinker, a bold investor, a challenge acceptor, and Blaine has NEVER been frightened by the idea of taking an idea, a product, or a service and investing time and money behind making it better.

There are not a lot of people I would be more thrilled to write this Trust Based Entrepreneur book with than Blaine because he has already succeeded and failed over and over again.

And…to be an AUTHORITY…you must have EXPERIENCED both!

You will be wise to listen to the WISDOM of a bold young Entrepreneur…introducing…my son Mark Blaine Given, Jr.

MARK BLAINE GIVEN, JR

GIVEN COACHING
FIND YOUR LIMITLESS POTENTIAL
www.givencoaching.com

PROVEN WAY #9

ENTREPRENEURS ARE GIVERS!

"The secret to living is giving!"

Tony Robbins

Throughout history those that have been respected and whose legacies live on, are those that gave! Many times, we associate giving with money, but that is not always the case. There are people that have crossed your path that you will be forever grateful for and made a huge impact on your life. What was their gift to you that made such the difference? You can do the same for others. Often entrepreneurship gives us the ability to assist in financial ways, but there is so much more to us than just our money! You have been given much! I have found the more I give, I get so much more in return! I cannot afford financially, physically, psychologically, or spiritually not to give! If you need to improve in this area, please make sure you are doing it for the right reasons. We all can tell when people's motives are not sincere!

How can you begin to give back in a different way than you have before? To whom can you give things more precious than money?

Lemonade FREE
Generous Donations Accepted
VLADO TRTIC
KRIKYS

GIVEN COACHING
FIND YOUR LIMITLESS POTENTIAL
www.givencoaching.com

PROVEN WAY #10

ENTREPRENEURS EMBRACE THE SUCK!

"Life sucks and then you die!"

Janice Given

Embrace the suck is a term that has been used for many years in the military and has now made its way into civilian life. It means to consciously accept or appreciate something that is extremely unpleasant but unavoidable. Life is full of these "somethings"! The difference that I have found between successful and unsuccessful entrepreneurs is their willingness to do and not avoid. I have never been in the military, but I have tremendous respect and admiration for those brave men and women. From my observations and my opinion, embracing the suck is something they begin doing at the beginning of their military career sand based upon their willingness to continue to embrace the suck, some go on to be elite specialists in different fields and forces. Are we willing to be "Special Forces" caliber entrepreneurs? It will depend on if we are willing to be determined and disciplined enough to do the frustrating and unpleasant things, instead of putting them off. Some of these things can be delegated and if you can, do it! Unfortunately, some things can only be completed by you. Have you heard of the phrase "eat the frog"? The interpretation of this is to tackle the most daunting and unpleasant task of the day first. So, don't *suck*, just *eat the frog*!

"Our culture has become hooked on the quick-fix, the life hack, efficiency. Everyone is on the hunt for that simple action algorithm that nets maximum profit with the least amount of effort. There's no denying this attitude may get you some of the trappings of success, if you're lucky, but it will not lead to a calloused mind or self-mastery. If you want to master the mind and remove your governor, you'll have to become addicted to hard work. Because passion and obsession, even talent, are only useful tools if you have the work ethic to back them up."

—David Goggins

What do you feel are some of your biggest *frogs*? How will you *embrace the suck* and eat those *frogs* first?

GIVEN COACHING
FIND YOUR LIMITLESS POTENTIAL
www.givencoaching.com

PROVEN WAY #11

ENTREPRENEURS INVENT SOLUTIONS FOR THEIR PROBLEMS

"A person who sees a problem is a human being: a person who finds a solution is visionary; and the person who goes out and does something about it is an entrepreneur."

Naveen Jain

There are some certainties to life as you've heard, death & taxes. Well, I have found that there is another and that is; problems. We all have them. Recently we have been plagued by a worldwide pandemic. It has forced many to close, sell, or just give up. For others it has created opportunities for them to be creative and find solutions and ways to keep paying the bills and to keep promises. For Janelle and me, it was taking an older movie screen that we had in storage and building a portable movie screen so that we could do "Pop-up Cinemas" for individuals, churches, schools, and other organizations. We did fundraisers and other events. Most went great and a couple were, in our opinion, epic failures. As entrepreneurs, we don't deal well with others controlling our destiny, so we make a way! Whatever the skills and talents that you have been given from God or the Universe, use them. Those brilliant business ideas you get in the bathroom or in the shower, act on them! Solve your problem because the solution can only be found within you.

"You are either part of the problem or part of the solution!"

Mark Blaine Given Jr.

What's Your challenge question here?

PROVEN WAY #12

ENTREPRENEURS INVENT SOLUTIONS FOR YOUR PROBLEMS

"There is opportunity in every obstacle!"

Mark Blaine Given Jr.

I have a friend that owns a tire and automotive shop. He is known for his hard work, dedication, and entrepreneurship! Recently his business was slightly down. He had been working with a third party that was providing his clients the ability to finance tires and auto repairs. After working with this company for about two years he thought, "I have some money with which to gamble. I'm willing to take some risk. Let me hire someone that I can trust and is willing to do the due diligence in making lending decisions and see what we can do." He saw that people would put off getting new tires, having repairs made, or accessorizing their vehicles all problems that he could help with, due to not having large sums of money at any given time. He watched people try to use the third party but because of their terms, clients would put off the expenditures. He saw this third-party company do what he felt was taking advantage of these individuals by charging them excessive interest. He and his team set up a weekly payment plan for these individuals and put it on draft and charged significantly less interest. He could charge less and still come out ahead due to the other incentives that were built in by suppliers. Within the first month he doubled his money both in revenue to the shop and the money he invested. The second month, he set record numbers for all aspects of his business. Now, it's important to note that a couple of months can be a little premature to celebrate a new fortune, but it can provide the ability to forecast. He saw a problem and found a solution. He already had his clients and customers trust and business. He has now found a way to increase that! Sometimes some people find solutions that are world changing and sometimes we find solutions that solve individual problems. Is one better than the other? One may be more financially rewarding but the other may be more rewarding in many ways. This has all been accomplished by my friend who dropped out of high school at 16. He went and earned his GED. He wanted to go into law enforcement and while he was in BLET, he started a part time job at a tire shop. He now has a booming business in a small town in North Carolina and makes people's dreams come true on a daily basis! To me he is a master inventor!

"Great entrepreneurs focus intensely on an opportunity where others see nothing"

Naveen Jain

What can you do to be the inventor that your current and future clients or customers need you to be? Name five talents that you have that make you unique in your world.

GIVEN COACHING
FIND YOUR LIMITLESS POTENTIAL
www.givencoaching.com

PROVEN WAY #13

ENTREPRENEURS ARE RAINMAKERS

"Be a rainmaker; the world has enough followers!"

Mark Blaine Given Jr.

A rainmaker is understood to be someone that is willing to perform tasks that make a big impact in a business that others cannot or are unwilling to do. For example, I own an insurance business and it is important that I make and keep a good relationship with our top clients. These clients I label as my "A" clients. These "A" clients may have large accounts. They may be networking keys. They may be influencers in the community. You decide who these "A" clients are. I can get stuck in the office taking payments and initiating changes, or I can add someone to my team that is amazing at that so that I can focus on building relationships that will build my business. I had a mentor once tell me, "You're stuck in the weeds. GET OUT!" My associates can and often do speak with, serve, and influence these individuals; however, there are times that you need to be the face. This is something with which you will need to find a happy balance. I do not want to be a prisoner to my business, but I don't want to be an absentee owner.

What do you think you could be doing now that will make a big impact for your current business or the business you plan to start?

PROVEN WAY #14

ENTREPRENEURS ARE WILLING TO SACRIFICE

Do you want a quote here?

Sacrifice is a word that brings strange emotions in our world. I have found that while success does require sacrifice, it doesn't always mean losing something important to you. If you want to change your income, then what are willing to sacrifice to do so? Maybe you might need to sacrifice your Netflix binge watching until midnight, so you can wake up early. Have you noticed when you wake up early your house is quiet and there are fewer distractions? Can you picture it? The time where the kids are still fast asleep, the phone isn't ringing and no one needs you for a short period of time. What would you do with that time? I have found this time can be great for meditating or praying. Reading good books or scriptures. Making or tweaking to do lists for the day. Could your sacrifice be packing your lunch so that you can stay at the office and get some things done a few times a week while others are out not maximizing their time? If you are the rain maker, then what makes the rain for you and your dream? Small sacrifices can make a huge difference. Jim Rohn said, *"If you are not willing to risk the unusual, you will have to settle for the ordinary."*

"You can only become great at things you are willing to sacrifice for."

—Maya Angela

Sacrificing the things that are most important to you in your personal life for financial or career success is like rewarding yourself with a candy bar for working out.

Do not sacrifice the most important things in your life in pursuit of what you think will bring you success and happiness! How often have you heard that people on their death bed wish they had spent more time with their loved ones? Go big at home and you will be amazed at the huge results that occur all around you!

What are 3 small things you could begin to sacrifice that could have a huge effect?

PROVEN WAY #15

ENTREPRENEURS ARE DOERS!

"The difference between who you are, who you want to be and the success you want to achieve is most affected by what you do!"

Mark Blaine Given Jr.

There are so many people, if not everyone, that have great ideas. There are many people that work for a company or do business with a company that see and talk about how things could or should be better. A big variable that exists between you and them, is that you are a doer. You don't just talk the talk but you walk the walk. Success comes when the team that you put together sees you doing the work and not just talking about it. You will be shocked at the buy in you will get from your entire team when they see you with a broom, wrench, hammer, pen, drill, or whatever the appropriate tool of your trade is.

"The way to get started is to quit talking and begin doing."

Walt Disney

"It is now time to *do it*."
Spencer W Kimball

What is something you need to change or pick up to show your team the "buy-in" you have for your business or idea?

Don't call them wishes, call them dreams of realities in waiting!

GIVEN COACHING
FIND YOUR LIMITLESS POTENTIAL
www.givencoaching.com

PROVEN WAY #16

ENTREPRENEURS ARE DREAMERS!

"All our dreams can come true if we have the courage to pursue them!"

Walt Disney

I love to watch my kids play. Their imaginations are amazing, and they get that from their magnificent mother! What causes us along the path to lose the ability to dream or use our imaginations? Some people still do dream and most think they are crazy! It would be an honor for me to be included with some of the crazies like Walt Disney, Steve Jobs, The Wright Brothers, Elon Musk, George Lucas and many more! My dreams may not have the effect on millions as these dreamers did, but I can still have an impact. I have found that Walt is right. If you can dream it and then you write it down, it is amazing what can happen. Writing dreams down, seems to create a force in the universe that causes unimaginable things to occur. But they aren't unimaginable to you! There is NO limit to what we can do and what we can dream!

"Do not put handcuffs on God or the universe, by being unwilling to dream big!"

Mark B Given Jr.

What are the dreams that you want God or the universe to begin working on for you? Try to list 4!

PROVEN WAY #17

ENTREPRENEURS ARE FLEXIBLE

"Flexible in the face of change, resilient in the face of confusion. All of these attributes are choices, not talents, and all of them are available to you."

Seth Godin

Dad discussed earlier the importance of being focused. That is super important, but it should not cause us to be rigid. Your business is like a river. It can flow, be blocked, and it can change direction if you are flexible. Do not fight the laws of nature or society or the other forces out there. Tony Robbins teaches, "Stay committed to your decisions, but stay flexible in your approach." It is important that you not eb and flow with the wind, but always fighting it is exhausting! You are the captain! Have confidence in your direction and listen to those you have aboard your ship. There is a reason you have them there. They may see things that need to which will be huge in navigating the waters ahead!

"Be committed and flexible... just like Elastigirl!"

Mark B Given Jr.

What is one way that you are willing to become more flexible?

PROVEN WAY #18

ENTREPRENEURS ARE LEARNERS

"You never lose in business, either you win or you learn."

Melinda Emerson

Zig Ziglar regularly encouraged those that learned from him to be involved in "Automobile University". Automobile University is using the time that you have in the car by yourself to learn and grow by listening to podcasts, books, Ted Talks, etc. Steven Covey taught the importance of sharpening your saw. Sharpening your saw according to Covey was the consistent pursuit of learning new things or advancing your knowledge on current areas of expertise. There are many individuals and businesses that you chose to do business with, why? Is it because you see them as experts? Can you tell, by their actions that they are actively involved in becoming better or are they just telling you they are? What is your definition of expert or better? Working to change others can be almost impossible, however changing or bettering ourselves can be very rewarding. I find great value in working to better myself in all aspects that are important to me and have a positive influence on those that surround me. We have access to so much information now due to apps and podcasts. There can be some good stuff on the radio, but there is immense knowledge in the devise in your pocket. There is more than likely a podcast on anything you would like to learn about. If not, start one! You can have almost any book delivered to you in a matter of days or instantly electronically.

"If you are unwilling to learn, no one can help! If you are intentional in learning, no one can stop you!"

Mark Blaine Given Jr.

How can you make better use of your time to keep learning and be unstoppable?

PROVEN WAY #19

ENTREPRENEURS SEE OPPORTUNITIES

"Opportunity is everywhere, and entrepreneurs have eyes to see it!"

Mark Blaine Given Jr.

We live in a world today that things happen fast! In our 21st century world we always have to have our antennas up! We, like every other person that have ever existed, have opportunities, but due to current ever changing technology, these opportunities for most in first world countries are very different. Many of these opportunities can be solved by technology, but many can't. What are your strengths? What are your talents? What are the opportunities you see in the world around you that others don't? How can you act and not get bogged down with paralysis by analysis? What causes you not to act or not to act fast enough to capitalize on your idea? Does the opportunity you see help many or just a few or just you? All can be very rewarding in all aspects. We currently have a global marketplace but also global competition. As entrepreneurs, we often have to act! You have years of experience behind you. When your gut says go for it, just go for it! The worst that can happen is that it doesn't go well, and you learn and move on. Failure or fear of failure often fuels entrepreneurs! I have personally learned much more from my mistakes than from my successes.

"Some see walls, entrepreneurs find the hidden doors!!

Mark Blaine Given Jr.

What are three ways that you can make sure you have your antennas up so you don't miss an opportunity?

MARK GIVEN

FINAL WORDS

TRUST BASED
PHILOSOPHY

TRUST BASED
ACADEMY

TRUST BASED
COACHING

PROVEN WAY #20

INTRAPRENEURS AND EXTRA-PRENEURS

Just recently, I came upon two additional groupings of Entrepreneurs, so after having read this book and considering the counsel and advice of three experienced Entrepreneurs, you may find that a better definition of what YOU are seeking is not Entrepreneur at all, but rather one of the following:

Intrapreneurs are defined as employees or staff of a company, association or organization who are assigned to complete special work or hired only to fulfill a special project.

They are given the time, freedom, and resources to complete the project.

They may use their own Entrepreneurial skills to develop and create, but ultimately the credit and ownership belongs to the company, association, or organization they work for.

In comparison, an **Entrepreneur** envisions and creates from the ground up, but the **Intrapreneur** broadens an already established idea, product or service using their personal experience or knowledge to make it better.

As an example, sometime in 1998 or 1999, as I was in the process of closing out my retail company, I was approached by, and considered working with, an already established financial advisor and educator. He had been running his business for nearly four decades and he wanted me to help him succeed through the next twenty years.

I did not accept his offer, but if I had, I would have given up ownership of any and all new ideas, products or services that I would create while in his employ (Intrapreneur).

I would create for him, but he would have the ownership of all that the ideas I would have wanted to believe was my new intellectual property.

Wisely, I choose not to go down that path and it has made a considerable difference in many of the decisions I made since that time.

As an example, the Trust Based Philosophy would never have been created and all the Trust Based books that have been written or will continue to be written would have never happened had I chosen to become an **Intrapreneur**.

For you though, it might be a safe haven and a wise choice. Less risk, no financial investment and potentially a guaranteed outcome.

A second new definition I found is called **Extra-preneur**.

An **Extra-preneur** is similar to an Intrapreneur in service, but they also apply their talents externally to other organizations, then use those experiences to bring back internally to the mother ship.

Here's what I believe is a good example.

Our youngest child and daughter Kerrilyn is a wonderful dance teacher and choreographer that works with my bride (Gigi). Kerri works very hard several days a week creating and teaching mostly children ages 5 – 19.

Two seasons ago, a rural elementary school near where she lives in NC asked Kerri if she could provide dance classes as part of their after-school curriculum.

Kerri then, working as an **Extra-preneur** traveled one day a week to the school for three or four months and provided the lessons they were seeking. She used many of the dances she had choregraphed as part of Given's Dance Studio, she used equipment and props from the studio for lessons each week and for the spring recital the kids performed in.

In a similar fashion to Kerri, you might find potential work as an **Extra-preneur** (assuming your employer would allow you to do so and you could negotiate the terms of your time and the information, intellectual property or service rendered).

"My grandfather once told me that there were two kinds of people: those who do the work and those who take the credit. He told me to try to be in the first group; there was much less competition."

Indira Gandhi

How could you use the concepts of Intrapreneur or Extrapreneur to improve your circumstances and your future?

TRUST BASED
PHILOSOPHY

That is a great idea, but it's never been done before.
What makes YOU think it will work?!

ONE LAST MESSAGE FROM MARK & BLAINE

THANK-YOU!

We each have seen it over and over…

"***Exceptional performance is only exceptional because of purposeful preparation***" and we are confident that you too have witnessed that to be true over and over.

We have also learned through personal experience and through watching people in many entrepreneur scenarios that the individuals who come prepared to maximize their opportunities walk away more successful than those that are not as prepared. If you show up ready to listen and learn and you're willing to do the work, you can't stop great things from happening. So…go make great things happen!

Trust in the process.

Why?

Because, when you do…God (and the Universe) will conspire to make success and achievement part of your life.

So…**Thank-You** for taking some of your valuable time to invest in YOU by reading this book…but reading is just the first step.

Now…you have to go out and actually apply it every day of your life.

You can do it and the time to start is right now!

I hope you know that we are just two people rooting for your success, so go get a piece of paper right now and write down where and how you're going to begin improving your life and business by adding these proven Trust principles.

And when it's convenient, drop us a note and let us know how it all worked out for you…your ENTREPRENUER success stories is important to us and we love hearing success stories!

You can reach us at:

Mark Given International
P.O. Box 1460
Roanoke Rapids, NC 27870
252-536-1169
mark@markgiven.com

Mark Blaine Given, Jr
2012 Stone Pasture Road
Fuquay Varina, NC 27526
252-578-6533
blainegiven@me.com

You might also consider making the world a little better by sharing this book with someone else. If you choose to not give it away, please know that you can purchase as many extra copies as you want or need through us or on Amazon.com!

You can reach Mark Given at:

mark@markgiven.com

www.markgiven.com

252-536-1169

You can reach Blaine Given at:

blainegiven@me.com

www.givencoaching.com

252-578-6533

BOOK BONUS

BOOK BONUS

10 MORE SECRETS OF SOUTHERN HOSPITALITY

1. **Pulling out the good china** – It seems today, we eat with paper plates and plastic utensils more and more often if we eat at home at all. And I guess that's easy to understand because most families I know eat out for most meals anyway. It is just easier and more convenient.

   But…there were times when pulling out the good china was the right choice and the right way to show how much we appreciate our guests.

   When I was young, all we ate on was real plates with real silverware and the good china was always on the table for special dates and special occasions. On any date, the more important the family member and for every important the holiday, the good stuff was on the placemat.

When I moved to the South, my Mother-In-Law had her china out every time we visited, and she had several sets she could use based on the circumstances. My wife has followed nicely in Mom El's shoes.

I guess it's pretty difficult today though when you don't own good china or any glass plates at all (I'm not sure that any of my five children do).

Nonetheless, if you ever experienced it, you know that the principle is true. It has always been that way in the South and it would not be a bad tradition for you to follow.

2. **Using good table manners** – I can't even imagine burping, farting or eating with my mouth open at the table. My daughter will give you the evil stare if you blow your nose at the table too.

   You don't sit down in your seat until all the women are seated and if your sister or your daughter or anybody's gal comes in late after you're seated, you'd be much better off to show your high level of Southern Gentlemanly habits and stand up and wait for those gals to be seated.

   Eat with your fork in your right hand and with the prongs facing up (you are not in Europe) and your table knife (if you use it) in your left hand. It's ok to scoop so go on and do it, but don't slurp…that's not ok.

   Do not reach across someone else's food to get that salt or barbeque sauce and always say please and thank-you for everything that you are given.

It is ok to feed your dog under the table or when they are sitting beside you, but don't throw him a bone or a piece of meat across the room.

And stop yelling at the kids while you're eatin'. Dinner time is a time for family love and gathering and sharing the days stories and lessons you've learned.

And finally, you may not have taken a bath, but it's never ok in the South to act or talk dirty at the dinner table (or any meal for matters) …it just ain't right!

3. **Waiting in line** – Of course you are in a hurry, everybody seems to be these days. And of course it's frustrating to have to wait.

   But…are you really that important? Are you really that special? Are you really that entitled to special treatment, way more than all the other people that are lined up waiting?

   I bet, whether you are from the South or not that you learned basic levels of respect and kindness way back in kindergarten (get in that straight line and wait your turn).

Being late or being impatient does not make you special. It does not mean you get to cut to the front of the line!

So back off…act with some responsible level of manners…get out your BEST Southern Hospitality Kindnesses and get in the back of the line just like everybody else did!

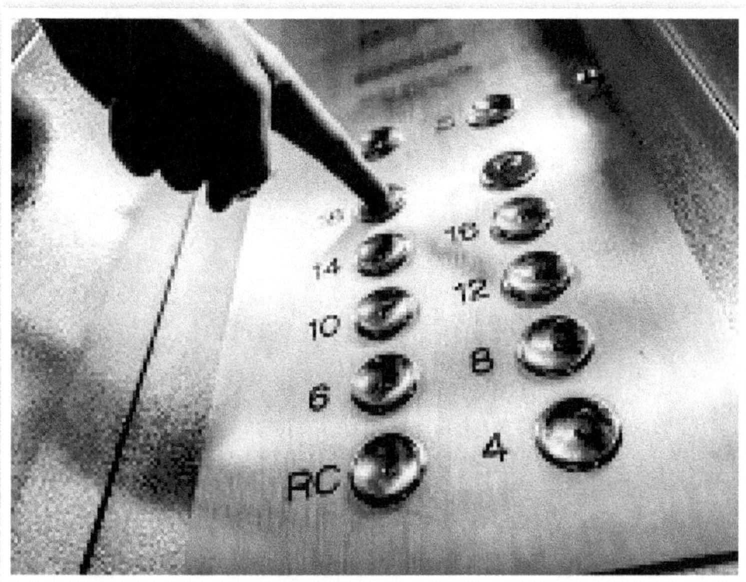

4. **Holding the elevator** – You've seen it done (I hope you weren't the one we witnessed doing it). Someone gets on the elevator, hits their floor button then immediately whacks at the door close button.

   If that is you…are you really in that big of hurry? Do you really have that big of phobia about a stranger sharing your space? Are you actually so entitled that YOU deserve your own elevator? Have you even looked to see if someone else is running to catch what you were so lucky to acquire?

   Next time pause for a moment and hold that elevator door. Let someone else in that is probably in a hurry too.

Who knows…that next time you show a little Southern Hospitality and welcome one more person on your golden elevator, it might just turn out to be a golden opportunity…and we all need more golden opportunities!

5. **Opening the door for women and men** – Kindness and politeness should not be gender specific and everyone appreciates not having a door slammed in their face. And…it is really not hard to do…just open the door.

   Why wouldn't you do that small kindness? You do not have to hold the door for the next dozen or so people, but one or two can help make your day.

   And if you're lucky, they might even say thank-you!

6. **Remembering the little words** – Please, thank-you, may I, you're welcome…these simple words really do matter. These words are the foundation of politeness and are basic social niceties. And…in my mind and in my experience, there is no really good excuse not to use them.

7. **Asking permission** – We live in a time and in a society that a motto seems to be "it's better to apologize than ask permission" but asking permission should be a no-brainer. And…we are wrong when we assume consent.

   So, before you go posting someone's picture online, or invading their personal space, or borrowing something because it's easier to just do it…stop and ask. That is just the right thing to do and your mother will be proud of you for doing it the right way.

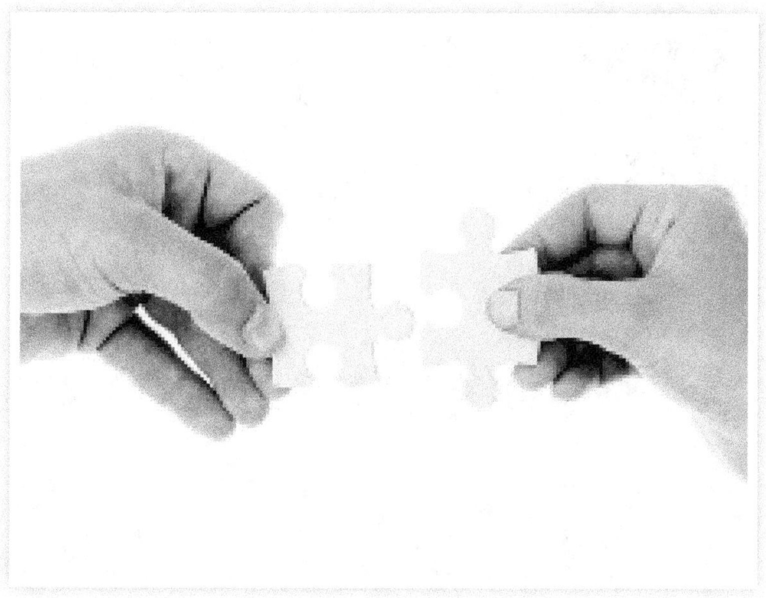

8. **Making introductions** – Making introductions is one of the most important social skills you can develop and yet, introducing others has become a lost art.

   Even when you have forgotten someone's name, it's better to ask them than to let that person stand in a group and be ignored. If you have ever experienced it, you know that a terribly empty feeling.

   Making an introduction is all about making someone else feel comfortable, welcomed, and valued no matter what the situation or what the surroundings.

   So, next time the opportunity presents itself, introduce your friend. You will feel better and they'll love you for it!

9. **Apologizing sincerely and in person** – When you've made a mistake (and we all do), the right thing to do is own up to it and apologize…in person.

   That may not be easy to do, but it is still what your mama' and your grandmama' would have you do.

   And…just in case you have not read any of the other Trust Based Philosophy books, here's the 4-step process to a proper apology:

   Recognize that you goofed

   Admit that you did something wrong and tell the person you harmed how you believe it made them feel.

   Tell them what you will do to rectify the situation and make it better.

   Promise that you will not do it again…then don't!

You cannot expect everyone to always accept your apology, but that is no reason to not take the high road and do the right thing.

Apologize…it is the only way to repair the damage you did and relieve your conscience!

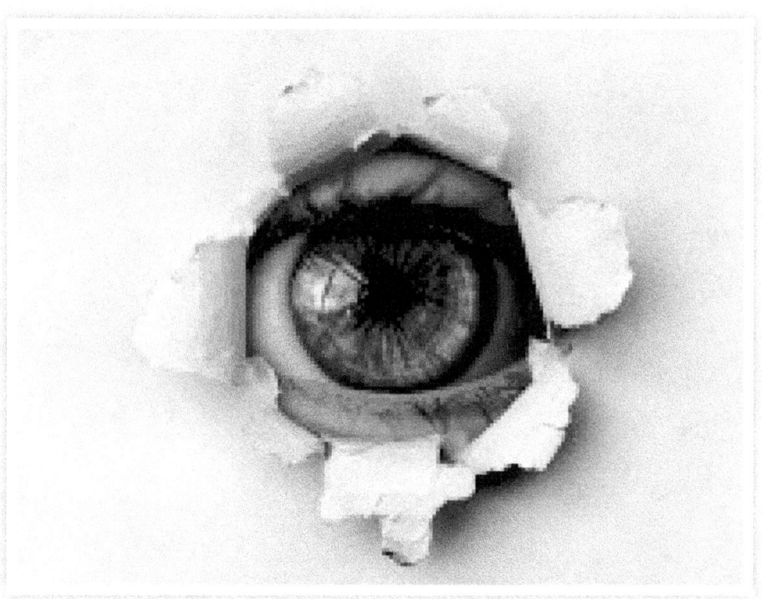

10. **Minding your own business** – Prime time TV may be full of it, social media may thrive on it, the checkout stand has magazines shouting it to everyone that will look, and some people just can't get enough of it…but…that doesn't mean you have too.

    Your grandma would want you to be more careful about what you say about another person, both in public and in private.

    And…not only is it polite to not speak about others behind their back, but you gotta' know that it's always better to take the high ground and never speak ill of anyone.

ADDITIONAL BONUS

MARK GIVEN INTERVIEWED BY KEVIN HARRINGTON

Original SHARK on ABC's Shark Tank and Inventor of the Infomercial

Kevin: Hi! I'm Kevin Harrington, an original shark from the hit TV show Shark Tank and I'm here with Mark given. He's a speaker, author…Here's his book *Trust Based Success*, coach. He goes all around the country speaking about his Trust Based Philosophy. Mark, I want to say thanks for being here.

Mark: My pleasure.

Kevin: We go back a number of years. In fact, I'm endorsing your book here and its very powerful what you're doing and getting so many speaking engagements is proof that what you're doing is landing in the marketplace. So, tell me how you got started with the Trust Based Philosophy.

Mark: Sure, my whole life has been about trying to be a trustworthy person and I realized that there is a science behind it.

Kevin: Right

Mark: It's not just a concept. So, I started studying it, understanding the science behind building, repairing trust, maintaining trust, how to create it and then fix it when there is a problem.

Kevin: Okay

Mark: And then, I've spent my whole life doing it.

Kevin: Does this work with husbands and wives too?

Mark: It does.

Kevin: Across the board.

Mark: It works for organizations, associations, but obviously I've had some people come to me

Kevin: You might keep some families together.

Mark: That's right. You know trust is such an important principle because our whole life and business begins when we establish trust and it crushes, it crumbles, it just all comes apart when we destroy trust.

Kevin: Yes

Mark: So, I spend my whole business life and my family life trying to help people understand not just what it is but how to do it. How to create trust.

Kevin: I love it.

Mark: And how to make it deeper and better.

Kevin: So, people out there who may be listening, they may be saying I think I already have some trust but it may not be powerful enough, deep enough or it may not be what they think either, right? So, it's got to be a mutual situation, right?

Mark: Sure, and as I travel and speak to organizations, associations and groups all over whether it be education or corporate, I actually teach them the four facets of trust which is there is a grand opening

Kevin: Right

Mark: We only get one opportunity to make a first impression

Kevin: Right

Mark: I teach people how to have a much better, more successful opening and then we teach the rapport building stage which is…

Kevin: You only get one chance to make a good impression.

Mark: Exactly!

Kevin: So that's got to be a trust

Mark: That's right but we've not all be taught the best way to do it. We've all been taught that its important but not how to do it. I teach people how to do that.

Kevin: Right

Mark: We teach the rapport building stage which is about learning to ask more questions and really listen

Kevin: Okay

Mark: And so you probe in a really good, interesting and sincere, transparent way. Then we teach the maintenance phase.

Kevin: Okay

Mark: Which is how to maintain it for a long period of time.

Kevin: Right, yup.

Mark: And then we tach the repair stage, the apology phase and how when we mess it up how do we fix it because we are all make mistakes.

Kevin: Yes, I love it. Now you have 4 different versions of the book.

Mark: I do.

Kevin: This is *Trust Based Success*. We have *Trust Based Selling* because for sales people…I mean I'm a Zig Ziglar fan and he was a big guy in this regard.

Mark: Yes

Kevin: *Trust Based Networking*. This goes to some of the direct selling world out there and what's the fourth?

Mark: *Trust Based Leadership*

Kevin: *Trust Based Leadership* is corporate type opportunities there. You're very passionate and I can just feel it sitting here and I love getting together with you. How come? Was there a point where you had some big learning about trust or how did you develop this whole concept?

Mark: That is a great question. After college, I got out and started my own company. I grew a retail company for about 20 years until I sold it.

Kevin: Okay, took some chips off the table.

Mark: That's right. I started with one little location and ended up with 47.

Kevin: Okay

Mark: What I learned was that as a leader, as an example that if the people who worked for me and with me if they didn't trust me well they would not do well.

Kevin: Right.

Mark: I learned that our customers and clients, if we didn't have trust with them then they didn't come back. It was one and done and we needed them to come back, do business, send us repeat and referral business, to recommend us to other people so I really started as a result of that studying how do we do this?

Kevin: Right

Mark: Instead of just I need to have more trust, well how do I create it? What I discovered is most of the books out there are on the concept of trust but not the science of trust and not how to do it.

Kevin: I gotcha

Mark: So, I started going to work trying to figure it out and as a result have written these books. I have more books coming out in this Trust Based Philosophy series.

Kevin: Love it.

Mark: It's an ongoing thing. I think I'll do it until I die.

Kevin: There you go. Well you know it's a four-step process and my mind is going right towards because the repair side because I'm thinking somebody knows they have a problem, you're a problem solver, right? You can teach people how to start from the opening relationship but sometimes people may come to you because they've had the issue where they need repair.

Mark: Sure

Kevin: So, does it start at any one of those points at some times and is repair the side where people say I need Mark now.

Mark: Actually, I have companies or people that will call me and say here's our problem.

Kevin: Right

Mark: Corporations have called me before and say, "Hey, we messed up what are the proper steps for us to go through? What should we be thinking about? We don't know what we don't know so help us know what we need to know."

Kevin: Gotcha

Mark: So, what we do is teach them the steps to a proper apology because social media today, Kevin, you know what that's like with the internet. It used to be that if you upset one person they might tell 100. Now you can upset one person and they tell hundreds of thousands of people, right?

Kevin: Right

Mark: So, we try and help them whether it be an individual or a company or organization, there is a proper way to go through an apology. You cannot force people, you can't make people accept your apology.

Kevin: Right

Mark: But to repair, to rebuild trust you've got to go through the proper steps to do that.

Kevin: Right

Mark: So, there is a science to it.

Kevin: Love it. I always love to find the unique aspect of what you're doing over others and I think you've just said it. You address the science of trust.

Mark: That's correct

Kevin: Whereas others have to talk about it but you've already uncovered the 4 steps and the science to repairing it at the very end if that's needed. What are the biggest challenges that companies are having in this world now. I mean, you talk about social media and the difference today vs. say ten years ago, how do people deal with these challenges that are out there in your world of trust.

Mark: Leadership is obviously a critical point because what you do is way more powerful than what you just see. Media, marketing can help drive attention but the truth is what you do is what creates the true perception. So, authenticity is what I'm saying. We teach a lot about what's your authentic passion, what is it you're really trying to do.

Kevin: Right

Mark: You may create a product but that is just what you do. What's the systems behind that so that people can want to do business with you. We just have the ability now to research anything. So, companies need to be more authentic. They need to be more transparent just like individuals do. People can see right through us.

Kevin: Yes, yes.

Mark: It doesn't take long at all.

Kevin: That is right. Fantastic. There are people out there – direct selling people, entrepreneurs, executives that might apply to one of these four books that you've got but how would you get some words of encouragement to those that are out there and maybe how they might be able to reach you also. Let's try and help those that are there now. Give some words of encouragement on the whole business of trust.

Mark: Sure. Obviously, I've made it easy for people to find me. We are actually creating a new program called the Trust Based Academy so you'll be able to find us that way. But just www.markgiven.com. I'm easy to find so if they just look up trust hopefully we've got the right triggers out there to find that it links back to me and if they just go to my website there is plenty of information on there about what it is, what we do and how to reach me and they can sign up for we have a weekly message that we send out.

Kevin: Okay so you have some free downloads and some free information.

Mark: Sure

Kevin: That is great. When I think of today's world, millennials for example what are they looking for? Authenticity, right?

Mark: That's correct

Kevin: You know I've been in the business of selling products direct to the consumer for almost 40 years. In the old days, it was hard sell. Today, the millennials don't want that hard sell. They want a trust-based relationship. They want authenticity and I think it's great to see that you're filling their needs at this point. Thanks for being here today and I just want to say let me have all four of these.

Mark: You bet

Kevin: I just want to say here we go. We've got Mark Given, Trust Based Philosophy. He's written great books. You've got to go to his website **www.MarkGiven.com** and check it all out. You're going to get some free information, some free downloads. This is really exciting. Mark, thanks for being here.

Mark: Thank you Kevin. My pleasure.

TRUST BASED
PHILOSOPHY

www.ingramcontent.com/pod-product-compliance
Lightning Source LLC
LaVergne TN
LVHW020644100826
845148LV00012B/2338

* 9 7 8 1 7 3 7 0 7 5 5 0 9 *